Three Conversations
about
Knowing

Three Conversations about Knowing

Jay F. Rosenberg

Hackett Publishing Company, Inc.
Indianapolis/Cambridge

Copyright © 2000 by Hackett Publishing Company, Inc.

06   05   04   03   02   01   00   1   2   3   4   5   6   7   8   9

For further information, please address
  Hackett Publishing Company, Inc.
  P.O. Box 44937
  Indianapolis, IN 46244-0937

  www.hackettpublishing.com

Cover and interior designs by Abigail Coyle.

Library of Congress Cataloging-in-Publication Data

Rosenberg, Jay F.
        Three conversations about knowing / Jay F. Rosenberg
            p.   cm.
        Includes bibliographical references.
        ISBN 0-87220-537-1—ISBN 0-87220-536-3 (paper)
        1. Knowledge, Theory of. 2. Imaginary conversations. I. Title

    BD161 .R66 2000
    121—dc21   00-035018

CONTENTS

THE FIRST CONVERSATION

(Gemma's room. GEMMA is working at her computer. SKIP knocks softly on the half-open door and enters without waiting for a response.)

GEMMA: *(reading from the screen)* "What do you know?"

SKIP: What?

GEMMA: "What do you know?" It's supposed to be the only question on the final examination at an ancient Chinese academy.

SKIP: Well, that would certainly be a short exam. You'd just have to turn in a blank sheet of paper with your name on it.

GEMMA: You mean that the only thing you know is your own name?

SKIP: No. I don't even think you know that. The name is just so that you'd get credit for knowing that you don't know anything at all.

GEMMA: Oh come now! I know lots of things. I know how to ride a bike, and speak German, and make lasagna. I know the Pythagorean Theorem and that 2+2=4. I know that electrons have a negative charge and that water is H_2O. I know that it's Tuesday, the sun is shining, the azaleas are in bloom, and we're both wearing blue shirts. And I certainly know my own name! I know all sorts of things. *Everyone* knows all sorts of things. What's hard about the ancient Chinese final exam is figuring out *which* of the many things that you know you ought to write down.

SKIP: Well, some of the things you claim to know you *couldn't* write down—how to speak German, for example. You probably couldn't write down how to ride a bike either, although you might be able to give someone a recipe for making lasagna.

GEMMA: I don't suppose that the ancient Chinese examiners would be interested in a recipe for lasagna.

SKIP: They probably weren't interested in any of the things their students knew *how* to do, except for whatever know-how it took to answer the exam question. Knowing how to speak German or ride a bike is just *being able* to do those things. It doesn't count as knowing any facts, as knowing *that something is the case*. I would have interpreted "What do you know?" as meaning "What do you know to be *true*?"—and that's why I would have turned in a blank sheet of paper.

GEMMA: But that's silly. Surely you also know all those facts I listed a minute ago—that 2+2=4, for instance, and that water is H_2O and the azaleas are in bloom, and so on. Why would you think otherwise? Surely you believe that all those things are true.

SKIP: Of course I *believe* all those things. I even agree that it would be silly not to believe them. But what I believe isn't what's at issue. The question is whether I *know* any of the vast number of things that I believe, and what I'm claiming is that I *don't*. I don't *know* any of them—and neither does anyone else.

GEMMA: Why not?

SKIP: Well, for different reasons, depending on what kind of belief we're talking about. You just mentioned three different kinds: mathematical beliefs, scientific beliefs involving theoretical entities, and ordinary perceptual beliefs. I'm afraid that the reasons I don't think anyone knows any mathematical facts are fairly complicated and technical. For one thing, I'm not convinced that there *are* any mathematical facts, because I'm not convinced that any of the things that mathematical beliefs seem to be *about*—numbers, sets,

points, lines, vectors, groups, or what have you—
actually exist. And if that's so, then mathematical
equations and other mathematical sentences might
very well not be in the business of "stating facts" at
all. For another thing, there are some technical results
in mathematical logic that suggest that we can never
be sure that any sufficiently complicated mathematical system, including ordinary arithmetic, doesn't con-
tain hidden contradictions. But all that gets difficult
and specialized pretty quickly, and rather than get tan-
gled up in such complications, I'm willing to concede, for the sake of argument, that people *do* know
that 2+2=4 and that the Pythagorean Theorem holds
for Euclidean right triangles, and other such relatively
straightforward mathematical claims. I doubt that the
ancient Chinese examiners would be more interested
in that kind of knowledge than in your recipe for
lasagna.

GEMMA: I think you're right. Besides, what's important in math
is also mostly a sort of know-how. If you're a mathe-
matician, you need to be able to prove things; if
you're a physicist, for example, you need to know
how to apply mathematical computations to what
you're measuring. Just knowing a bunch of mathematical facts isn't of much use. Math is more like a
tool. You have to be able to *do things* with it. But what
about the other sorts of beliefs we've mentioned?

SKIP: Well, to begin with, I'm not fully convinced that there
are such things as electrons or molecules any more
than I'm convinced that there are points or numbers.
After all, we never actually *meet* any of those things.
All that theoretical talk might just be a convenient
shorthand for summarizing and reasoning about the
things we *do* apparently encounter—glass rods rubbed
with fur and buckets of water, for instance—and about
the behavior of various scientific instruments: volt
meters, cloud chambers, electrolysis devices, and the
like. But, in any case, if we *do* know any facts about
such theoretical entities, we know them only *indirectly*, by reasoning and theorizing about the things we

seem to perceive directly. If we don't know that any of our ordinary perceptual beliefs are true, then, we don't know that any of our scientific theoretical beliefs are true either—and, as I've said, I also hold that we don't know that any of our ordinary perceptual beliefs are true.

GEMMA: OK, I can understand how someone could be skeptical about theoretical scientific beliefs. But I can't understand your reluctance to concede that you know such things as that the azaleas are in bloom or that I'm wearing a blue shirt. You can just *look* and *see* that these things are so, can't you?

SKIP: I'll concede that that's certainly how things *seem*. But perceptual experience is hardly infallible. An oar lowered into the river and a swizzle stick standing in a cocktail *look* bent, but we believe that they're really straight, and when I'm out driving on a warm summer day, it often looks like there's a puddle of water in the road ahead of me when it turns out that there isn't. And such illusions aren't limited to the sense of sight. No doubt you can think of lots of similar examples involving the other senses yourself.

GEMMA: Of course I can. But when I do, I also recognize that these sorts of illusions are very infrequent and occur only in special and unusual conditions. Take the oar out of the water or the swizzle stick out of the cocktail, and they'll look as straight as they in fact are. And when I actually arrive at the point in the road where it looked like there was a puddle of water, it doesn't look that way any more. In fact, that's how we know that such illusions occur in the first place. We can compare our visual experiences with our other sensory experiences—the oar *feels* straight even when it looks bent—or we can simply go take a closer look. And, of course, we can always ask other people how it looks to them.

SKIP: I'm not sure how asking other people is supposed to help. The oar and the swizzle stick look bent to every-

one, don't they? And everyone in the car sees the puddle of water mirage at the same time.

GEMMA: I was thinking more of hallucinations. If it seems to
me that there are orange ostriches dancing in the corner, it's more likely that someone has slipped me
some psychedelic drug than that the ostriches are
actually there. But if they *are* actually there, then
other people will be able to see them, too, and we'll
also all be able to hear them, smell them, and, if we
get close enough, touch them.

SKIP: Perhaps. But what if those other people are as unreal
as the dancing ostriches?

GEMMA: What do you mean?

SKIP: I mean that your beliefs about other people are just
more perceptual beliefs. If you can't rely on your own
perceptual beliefs to settle questions about what the
world is in fact like, then you can't know even that
there *are* other people, much less what they see and
hear and smell. Of course, the reasonable thing to
believe is that there are plenty of other people, and
that they generally see and hear and smell the same
things that you do in given circumstances. But you
mustn't forget that the question is whether you *know*
that any perceptual beliefs are true, and it's no good
assuming that *some* of them are, namely, your beliefs
about other people, in order to argue for or against
the truth of others.

GEMMA: But how could anyone be mistaken about something
like whether or not there are other people? There are
some situations in which I just *can't* go wrong. For
instance, how could I possibly doubt that you and I
are sitting here together, in front of my computer,
wearing blue T-shirts and discussing a weird old Chinese examination question?

SKIP: The French philosopher René Descartes thought of a
way about 350 years ago: You might be *dreaming* the

whole thing. It might seem to you that you are seated beside me in front of a computer, that we're both wearing blue shirts, and so on, while in reality you're wearing a nightgown and lying in your bed asleep. Sometimes one dreams such things in vivid and realistic detail. This could be one of those times.

GEMMA: So what you're saying is . . .

SKIP: That you can't rule out the possibility that you're dreaming. You don't know that you're not dreaming. But you would know that you're wearing a blue shirt, for example, only if you *did* know that you're not dreaming. So you don't know that you're wearing a blue shirt—or that any of the other things that seem to you to be true actually are true.

GEMMA: Well, I agree with you that *if* I can't rule out the possibility that I'm dreaming, then I don't know that we're sitting by my computer, wearing blue shirts, and having this conversation. But it seems perfectly obvious that I *can* rule out the possibility that I'm dreaming. For one thing, I clearly remember *waking up* earlier this morning. I had a bagel with cream cheese for breakfast and went for a mile run. Then I came back, showered, and settled down in front of the computer to read my e-mail. That's when you came wandering in.

SKIP: I'm not sure how all that is supposed to show that you're not dreaming. Is it because you seem to remember waking up? Haven't you ever *dreamed* that you woke up—and then later *really* woken up and realized that you'd only dreamed it? You've got to admit that that's at least possible.

GEMMA: I don't think I've ever dreamed anything like that—but I guess it is possible. I can't see any reason why someone couldn't have a dream like that. But what counts isn't just that I remember waking up. It's that my waking up was a part of my regular life. I wake up every morning. I often have a bagel for breakfast, I go for a mile run three or four days a week, and I try to check my e-mail every morning. Dreams don't hang together with ordinary life in that way. In dreams, anything can happen. Sometimes I dream that I can fly, or that I'm an astronaut, or dating a movie star. But those things don't happen in real life.

SKIP: And how do you know *that*? Look at it this way: When you dream that you're an astronaut, you're dreaming that *that's* your regular life. If you're dreaming that you're blasting off in the space shuttle, it'll be part of your dream that you woke up in Cape Canaveral, that you drank Tang with your breakfast, that you got suited up in your space gear, and so on. And when you dream that you can fly, you're dreaming that you can fly *in real life*. A dream is a "package deal". Seeming to remember things and believing that certain things belong to your normal life or have always been true are part of the *contents* of the dream, just as seeming to see, hear, and smell things are parts of its contents. That's why you can never rule out the possibility that you're dreaming.

GEMMA: I'm not convinced that dreams ever are such "package deals". Mine don't seem to be. Besides, if you're right, and we can't tell whether we're dreaming or awake, how would we *know* that dreams are "package deals"? How would we even know that there *are* such things as dreams? Your argument seems to be self-defeating.

SKIP: What do you mean?

GEMMA: You start by saying that there are these two different possibilities—a person can be awake and perceiving things or asleep and dreaming that he perceives things. But then you claim that there's no way to tell the two different possibilities apart. So what entitles you to say that there are two different possibilities in the first place? Unless you could distinguish being awake and perceiving from being asleep and dreaming, you couldn't know that they were *different* possibilities.

SKIP: No. You're confusing two notions of 'distinguishing'. All that I need in order to be entitled to talk about two different possibilities is to be able to say what the difference between perceiving and dreaming *is*—and I can do that. When I'm awake and perceiving, my experiences are *caused by* the very things they're *about*. For instance, if I'm actually seeing a blue shirt, my visual experience is caused by a blue shirt; if I'm hearing a barking dog, my auditory experience is caused by a dog's barking; and so on. If I'm merely *dreaming* of a blue shirt or a barking dog, however, I have the same *kinds* of experiences but they're *caused* in some other, abnormal way. Remember what Scrooge said to the ghost of Marley when he was convinced it was just a dream: "You may be an undigested bit of beef, a blot of mustard, a crumb of cheese, a fragment of underdone potato." In other words, perceiving and dreaming are different, so to speak, by definition, and so there's no problem about talking about two different possibilities. I can easily *describe* what the difference is.

What I agree with Descartes about is that no one can distinguish being awake from being asleep in the sense of being able to *tell* which of the two sorts of experiences he is having *here and now*. Being able to describe a difference between two kinds of experiences is one thing; being able to identify one's present experiences as being of this kind or that kind is something else. For that, it's not enough to know what the words 'perceiving' and 'dreaming' *mean*. There also needs to be something about the content of the experience itself to serve as a sign that it's one kind or the other, and that's just what we haven't got. What makes dream experiences different from waking experiences isn't anything about their contents; it's something about their causes. The *contents* of a dream experience can be indistinguishable from the contents of a waking experience.

GEMMA: Well, so you say. But I'm still not convinced that dreams are the right sort of "package deal" for that to be true.

SKIP: It doesn't have to be dreams, you know. That was just Descartes' suggestion. Nowadays we can tell science fiction stories instead. Consider, for instance, the possibility that you're only a brain in a vat, and that everything you're experiencing is just "virtual reality," caused by a stream of electrical stimuli from a sophisticated computer. Unless you can rule out that possibility, you can't know that any of your experiences "tell it like it is"—and so you can't know that you're sitting with me in front of your computer, or that we're both wearing blue T-shirts and having a conversation, just as we concluded earlier.

GEMMA: You mean, just as *you* concluded earlier. *I'm* still convinced that I know perfectly well that we're sitting in front of my computer, wearing blue T-shirts, and having a conversation. In fact, *because* I know that, I *can* rule out the possibility that I'm just a brain in a vat. My argument is just the reverse of yours: If I couldn't rule out the brain-in-a-vat scenario, I couldn't know what my present situation is; I *do* know what my present situation is; so I *can* rule out that scenario.

SKIP: But that just begs the question!

GEMMA: No it doesn't. You haven't given me any reason at all for doubting any of those ordinary, commonsensical things that we've been talking about, and, until you do, I'm entitled to claim that I know them to be true, in fact, that it's quite *certain* that they're true.

SKIP: But what about the possibility that you're only a brain in a vat, experiencing a virtual reality? Surely you'd believe exactly the same things in that case, and be just as certain that you knew them to be true.

GEMMA: Perhaps I would. Who knows what I would believe if I were a brain in a vat! That would at least depend on whether or not I *knew* that I was a brain in a vat. I might remember having agreed to become one, for instance. But even if I grant that you've described a possibility, that's *all* it is—a mere possibility. There's no reason at all for me to believe that it's actually the case, that I actually *am* a brain in a vat, and so no reason at all for me to worry about whether the various commonsensical things I believe about the world and about my present situation in it are false. Mere possibilities aren't reasons for doubting anything. Even if it's true that I *wouldn't* know that I was a brain in a vat if I *were* one, it doesn't follow that I don't *in fact* know right now that I'm *not* one—and that's one of the things I'm quite certain I *do* know.

Besides, I don't think it's even *possible* that I'm a brain in a vat, experiencing a computer-produced virtual reality. Our medical and computer technologies just aren't sophisticated enough. We haven't yet developed sufficiently advanced techniques and apparatus even for sustaining the biological functions of a disconnected human brain in the laboratory, much less computers and programs capable of controlling all of a person's sensory experiences down to the finest detail.

SKIP: Maybe it just *seems* to you that current technology isn't up to the job. But, in any case, it's clearly a *possible* scenario. One can describe it without contradicting oneself.

GEMMA: Well, if that's all you mean by 'possible', then I'll grant that it's a possible scenario. It's *logically* possible, in the sense that one can imagine it without violating any principles or laws of logic. But that's not sufficient to show that it's a *real* possibility, something that could actually be the case in *our* world. It's logically possible, I suppose, for someone to fly simply by flapping his arms, but that's not a real possibility in our world. It might not violate any laws of logic, but it would obviously violate some laws of nature. I'm not at all sure that your brain-in-a-vat scenario isn't like that, but even if it isn't, it's still not a *practical* possibility. Even if it's a *real* possibility, that is, it's not a *realistic* one. It's simply not within the scope of our current medical and computer expertise. And only real and realistic possibilities could count as actual reasons for doubting what we in fact know to be the case.

SKIP: There you go, begging the question again. You claim to know all sorts of things about the current state of medical and computer technology. But if you know anything about that stuff, you know it on the basis of ordinary perceptual experiences and memories, and they're not adequate for knowledge. It isn't important whether the brain-in-a-vat scenario is what you call a realistic possibility or even a real one. The *point* of such examples is only to dramatically illustrate the fact that there's no way to determine whether any given experience corresponds to the world simply by examining the contents of that experience. Now what you *believe* on the basis of an experience depends on its contents, but whether what you believe is *true* depends on the way the world actually is. You believe that you had a bagel for breakfast today because that's what it now *seems* to you that you remember, but your belief isn't true unless the bagel-eating that's represented in your seeming memory actually occurred. You believe that you're sitting next to someone who's wearing a blue shirt, because that's what it now *seems* to you that you see, but your belief isn't true unless I actually am in fact wearing a blue shirt. All you ever have to go on are the contents of your experiences—what you here and now *seem* to see, *seem* to hear, *seem* to remember, and so on—and so you can't ever be certain that any of the beliefs that you base on those experiences are true. But knowledge requires such certainty. You can't know something unless you're certain that it's true. So you don't really *know* what you had for breakfast this morning or whether there's actually a blue shirt in your immediate vicinity.

GEMMA: I agree with you about one thing, that knowledge requires certainty. It wouldn't make sense for me to say, for instance, "I know that I had a bagel for breakfast today, but I'm not certain what I had for breakfast today."

SKIP: Well, there you are! Something is certain only if there's no possible way to be mistaken about it, and you can't deny that you might be mistaken about what you had for breakfast today, can you? So you can't be certain that you had a bagel for breakfast today.

GEMMA: Of course I can. Something is certain just in case there's no actual reason to doubt it, and I have no reason to doubt that I had a bagel for breakfast today. I remember quite clearly slicing it, toasting it, spreading on the cream cheese, and then eating it.

SKIP: I've already conceded that that's the way it *seems* to you. That's what you *think* you remember. But, for all you *know*, your apparent memory is false, and you're making a mistake. Your memory isn't perfect. All you can be certain about is what here and now *seems* to you to be true.

GEMMA: I can't deny that I might be mistaken about *some* of the things I seem to remember. My memory certainly isn't infallible. I'm not terribly good with telephone numbers, for example. I *think* I remember your home number, but I'd have to confess that, even though I've called you at home lots of times, I'm still not entirely sure that I have it right. I wouldn't claim to know it by heart. But I don't just *think* that I remember having a bagel for breakfast today; it doesn't just *seem* to me that I remember it. I *do* remember it. The fact that my memory isn't infallible implies that I could be mistaken about some of the things I seem to remember, but it doesn't imply that I could be mistaken about *that*. It isn't the sort of thing that I sometimes get wrong—like telephone numbers or things that happened to me a long time ago.

(z enters.)

JUSTIN: What are you two arguing about? I could hear you halfway down the hall.

GEMMA: About how to answer an ancient Chinese final examination question.

JUSTIN: *What?*

SKIP: That's only how it got started. But we're not really arguing. We just disagree about how much it's possible to know about the world. Gemma thinks that she knows all sorts of things—that the azaleas are in bloom, that she and I are both wearing blue T-shirts, that she had a bagel for breakfast this morning, and so on. I'm convinced that she *believes* all those things. Why not? I believe them, too. I even agree that it would be silly and unreasonable not to believe them. But I don't think that either of us strictly speaking *knows* any of them.

GEMMA: That's because Skip thinks that you can't know anything unless you can rule out absolutely every possible way you could be mistaken about it, including dreams and far-fetched science-fiction scenarios. Consequently, on his view, the only thing you can know is how things *appear* to you. In contrast, I think that there's no problem about my knowing *lots* of things, including the fact that I'm *not* asleep and dreaming or a deluded brain in a vat. To know for certain that something is true, all one needs to do is eliminate any realistic grounds for doubting it. Since there's no reason to suppose that either my eyesight or my memory is defective, I conclude that I not only know how things *appear* to me, I also typically know how things *are*, for instance, that the azaleas are blooming, that I ate a bagel with cream cheese for breakfast, and that Skip and I are both wearing blue shirts.

JUSTIN: Let me get this straight. You're disagreeing about whether you're both wearing blue shirts?

GEMMA: No. We agree about *that*. If you asked either of us what color shirts we were wearing, we'd both say 'blue'. Neither of us actually doubts that for a minute.

JUSTIN: So what you're disagreeing about is only whether it's OK to say that you *know* that. You're disagreeing about the word 'know'.

SKIP: No. That's not quite it either. If we're speaking casually, I think it's probably OK to *say* that we both know that we're both wearing blue shirts. There is a loose, everyday sense of the word 'know' that just indicates that a person is confident about what she believes and can convincingly say *why* she believes it. It rules out the possibility, for instance, that she's just *guessing*. Neither of us is just guessing what color shirts we're wearing. It looks to both of us as if we're wearing blue ones, and, as we normally do, we trust our own eyes. That's why we both believe what we do, and that's why it's reasonable for us to believe it and would be silly not to. Now in such circumstances, people often *say* that they "know" whatever it is that they believe, and I'm prepared to grant that they're not exactly *misusing* the word 'know'. In ordinary circumstances, that's the appropriate thing to *say*. It would be misleading to say something like, "Well, both shirts look blue, and I'm inclined to think that they are, but I don't know for sure." That might lead people to suppose that there's something peculiar about me or my circumstances—that I may be colorblind or the lighting is odd or whatever.

But what got us started on this conversation was supposed to be a question on a *final exam*—"What do you know?"—and that's a context where speaking casually and loosely is *in*appropriate. The question in that case isn't whether it's OK to *say* that we know, for instance, that we're both wearing blue shirts, but whether it's strictly speaking *true* that we know that. And that's where Gemma and I part company. *She* thinks that the very same facts that make it appropriate in ordinary contexts to *say* that she knows are sufficient to make it literally *true* that she knows, but that seems to me to be obviously wrong.

JUSTIN: Why do you think so?

SKIP: Well, take the example of someone who buys a ticket
           in the state lottery. She certainly *hopes* that she's going
           to win the big jackpot—that's why she buys the
           ticket—but she's also well aware that the odds are
           vastly against her, about 15 million to 1, if I remem-
           ber rightly. So what's it reasonable for her to *believe*?
           Obviously, that she *won't* win the big jackpot. It's
           reasonable for her to believe that she won't win it, and
           it would be silly of her to believe that she will. If she's
           speaking loosely and casually, in fact, she might even
           express that reasonable belief by saying "Of course,
           I know that I won't ever actually win the big jackpot,
           but I still enjoy playing. There's that wonderful
           moment of suspense before the drawing." But strictly
           speaking, she obviously *doesn't* know that she won't
           win, and she doesn't know it precisely because she
           can't rule out the possibility that her numbers will be
           drawn.

JUSTIN: OK. I agree that she doesn't know that she's not going
           to win. If she actually knew that—if she knew that the
           lottery was dishonest and the winner was determined
           in advance, for example—then she wouldn't buy a
           ticket in the first place. But how does that show that
           you don't know what color shirts you and Gemma are
           wearing?

SKIP: We need one more step. You'll surely agree, too, that
           it doesn't make any difference how long the odds are,
           that is, how many tickets are in the lottery? If the odds
           were 15 *billion* to 1, for instance, the probability that
           her single ticket would be the winner would be only
           1/1000th of what it is when they're 15 million to 1.
           It would then be a thousand times more reasonable
           for her to believe that she wasn't going to win, and a
           thousand times sillier for her to believe that she would
           win. But it would still be true that she *could* win, and
           as long as she can't rule out that possibility—as long
           as there's *any chance at all* that she will win—then
           strictly speaking she doesn't *know* that she won't.

JUSTIN: Yes, I agree. It doesn't make any difference how many tickets there are. If it's a fair lottery with a random drawing, then no one knows in advance how it's going to turn out, and so none of the ticket holders knows whether or not she's going to win.

SKIP: So it can be clearly reasonable for someone to believe something and very improbable that she's mistaken about it and silly for her to doubt it, but as long as there's *any chance at all* she's mistaken, she doesn't strictly speaking know it. But that's just Gemma's and my own situation with regard to the color of our shirts! It's clearly reasonable for us to believe that they're both blue and very improbable that we're mistaken about that and silly for us to doubt it. But we're not infallible. There's always *some* chance, however small, that we *are* mistaken about it, and since that's so, then, strictly speaking, neither of us knows that we're both wearing blue shirts.

JUSTIN: Hmmm. I don't like your conclusion, but I can't off hand see what's wrong with your argument.

GEMMA: But there's got to be something wrong with it. If it's probabilities you want, then it's more likely that Skip has made a mistake in his reasoning than that we've made a mistake about what color shirts we're wearing.

SKIP: I'm not claiming that I *know* that my argument is a good one and my conclusion correct, only that that's the reasonable thing to believe.

GEMMA: I don't see what that has to do with what I just said.

JUSTIN: Skip's just applying his conclusion to his own argument. He's conceding that there's *some* chance that he's made a mistake in his reasoning, but, according to his argument, that doesn't show that it isn't reasonable to accept the reasoning and grant its conclusion. It only shows that we don't strictly speaking know that the conclusion is correct.

GEMMA: But that misses my point. What I claim is that it's *more* likely that Skip is mistaken than that his conclusion is true, and, if that's right, then since it's obviously reasonable to believe that we *do* know what color shirts we're wearing, it's *not* reasonable to accept Skip's argument at the same time.

JUSTIN: That may be so, but it doesn't help me out with my problem. You obviously agree that there's likely to be something wrong with Skip's argument. But even if I accept your claim that it's *more* likely that his reasoning is flawed than that his conclusion is true, I can't just *ignore* his argument. Until I can see just *what* is wrong with it, until I can say just what the flaw *is*, I really don't know what to believe. I need some time to think about it.

SKIP: Then take some time. I've got to get to class anyway—and so do you, Gemma. Listen. I'm meeting Edie for lunch at the Commons today, and I know that she's interested in this sort of stuff. Why don't you two join us, and we can take it from there. Maybe you'll have figured out what you want to say about my argument by then, Justin. How about it?

JUSTIN: Sounds good. I'll be there. Gemma?

GEMMA: I wouldn't miss it for the world. It's a date.

THE SECOND CONVERSATION

(Lunch at the Commons. SKIP, GEMMA, and EDIE are already sitting together at a table. JUSTIN comes over with his tray and joins them.)

JUSTIN: There you are. Have you filled Edie in on this morning's conversation?

EDIE: I think I've got the gist of it. Skip's been arguing that, strictly speaking, we know very little or nothing at all. To avoid complicated technicalities, he's prepared to grant that we do know mathematical truths—that 2+2=4 and that the sum of the interior angles of a Euclidean triangle is two right angles and so on—even speaking strictly. But he insists that we don't literally know any of the innumerable things *about the world* that we normally take ourselves to know. Gemma, on the other hand, has been valiantly defending the commonsensical view that we *of course* know all sorts of things about the world and our relationship to it, and that it would be silly to deny that we do. And you've been trying to figure out just what their disagreement actually amounts to, since both Skip and Gemma evidently agree that it's entirely reasonable to *believe* just about everything that we do in fact believe about the world, and Skip even concedes that there's a use of the word 'know'—he calls it a "casual" and "loose" use—according to which it's not mistaken to say that we know those things.

SKIP: Not quite. It is mistaken, but it's not inappropriate. You're not *misusing* the word 'know' if you apply it to that sort of situation, as you would be if you applied it to a case in which someone was just guessing.

EDIE: I sit corrected.

JUSTIN: And did Skip tell you his argument about the lottery tickets?

EDIE: That he did, and it certainly seems like a compelling one. You really don't want to say that the holder of a single ticket in a million or billion ticket lottery *knows* that she's not going to win, however reasonable it may be for her to believe that, do you?

JUSTIN: No, I don't—but that's not all there is to the argument, and I think I've figured out where the rest of it goes wrong. Skip supposes that the *reason* it's correct to say that the ticket holder doesn't know she's going to win is that there's always some small chance that her number will be drawn, and so some small chance that her belief that she won't win is mistaken. Since there's also some minuscule chance that Gemma and I are mistaken about, for instance, whether my shirt is blue, he concludes that we don't know that either.

SKIP: And where do you think that goes wrong?

JUSTIN: You're wrong about *why* the ticket holder doesn't know that she's not going to win. It's because the truth or falsehood of that belief depends upon a *random event* that hasn't yet occurred. But that's not the case with our normal beliefs about the world. Their truth or falsehood doesn't depend on such random events.

EDIE: It doesn't make any difference that the lottery drawing hasn't yet occurred, does it? I mean, if the drawing took place yesterday, but the results haven't yet been announced, the ticket holder could just as reasonably believe that she *hadn't* won, but, even if she's right, she still wouldn't know it, would she?

JUSTIN: No. It's the random factor that cancels out the possibility of knowing. But maybe the reason it's so much easier to know what has happened in the past than what will happen in the future is that there's still room for random events to intervene between now and some future time.

SKIP: I'm not convinced that randomness makes a difference. The fact that it's a random drawing explains why it's so improbable that any one ticket will be a winner, but it's the possibility of being mistaken that counts against knowing. Besides, there's a random factor in all sorts of ordinary beliefs. For instance, do you know where your car is?

JUSTIN: Sure I do. It's in the parking lot behind the library, where I left it this morning.

SKIP: It's certainly reasonable for you to believe that, and it's very probably true, but you've got to agree that you *might* be mistaken. Your car could have been stolen, for instance.

JUSTIN: Well, yes, it *could* have been. But there's no reason to believe that it *has* been. My belief about my car is nothing like the lottery ticket case.

SKIP: Now you sound like Gemma. But in fact it's *exactly* like the lottery ticket case. We all believe that there are car thieves out there, and that, on any given day, a certain number of cars will be stolen. So any time you park your car in a publicly accessible place, you're buying a ticket in the great stolen car lottery— although in this case, instead of hoping that your number will be drawn, you're hoping that it *won't* be. The rest of the argument goes through the same way, however. It's highly improbable that your car has been stolen today, and it's entirely reasonable for you to believe that it hasn't been and that it's still parked behind the library, but there's still some chance, however small, that your number has come up in the great stolen car lottery and that you're mistaken. So, strictly speaking, you don't know where your car is.

EDIE: Sounds like he's got you.

JUSTIN: No he doesn't. Cars aren't stolen at random. Car thieves have reasons for selecting which cars to steal. My eleven-year-old two-door compact isn't even close to being a tempting target. It doesn't even have a decent radio. There's no way any sensible thief is going to pick my car to steal. So I *do* know where my car is—behind the library, where I parked it.

SKIP: But you can't be *certain* that it's still there. Maybe no sensible thief would pick it, but not all thieves are sensible. Some kid who wanted to go joyriding might just have taken it on a whim. You can't absolutely rule out the possibility that you car's been stolen, and as long as there's any chance, however small, that you're mistaken about where it is, you don't know where it is.

JUSTIN: Well, that's a point on which I disagree with both you and Gemma. Evidently you both think that knowledge requires certainty. You argue that we can't ever be absolutely certain that any of our beliefs about the world are true, so we don't strictly speaking know anything about the world. Gemma argues that we do know a great deal about the world, and consequently, we can be certain that many of the things that we believe about the world are true. But I don't think that knowledge and certainty go together that way at all. I think that we can and do know lots of things about the world—what color shirt you're wearing, for instance, or where my car is—without being *certain* of the truth of any of it, that is, without having to say that there's no chance that we're mistaken.

GEMMA: But you've got to grant that there's something wrong about saying, for instance, "I know where my car is at the moment, but I'm not absolutely certain where it is" or "I know where my car is, but I might be mistaken about where it is."

JUSTIN: I'll grant that there's something peculiar about *saying* such things, but I won't grant that they couldn't be true. What makes it peculiar is that when we say things we also often express various attitudes. When I *say* "I know where my car is," then among other things, I express confidence that my belief that my car is parked behind the library is true. If I *say* "I'm not absolutely certain where my car is" or "I might be mistaken about where my car is," on the other hand, then I express a *lack* of such confidence in the truth of my beliefs about the location of my car. That makes it inappropriate and so peculiar to *say* both things at the same time—but it doesn't follow that it can't be *true* at the same time both that I know where my car is and that I can't rule out every possibility of being mistaken, however remote, and hence that I'm not absolutely certain about where it is.

SKIP: But knowing *excludes* the possibility of being mistaken!

JUSTIN: That depends on what you mean. If you mean that someone can't both know something and be mistaken about it at the same time, you're absolutely right. Only *true* beliefs can qualify as knowledge. You can believe what isn't the case, but you can't know what isn't the case, and so, if you *are* mistaken, then you don't know. But if you mean that it can't be the case that anyone knows anything that it's possible for him to be mistaken about, then I disagree. Knowing something is incompatible with *actually* being mistaken about it, but not with the mere possibility that one is mistaken. Gemma's right about that much.

SKIP: Well, I'm still not convinced. But just what do *you* think it takes in order to know something?

JUSTIN: We're still talking about matter-of-factual knowledge about the world, right? Then I would say that someone knows something—let's call it 'K'—just in case he *believes* that K is the case; and K *is* the case, that is, what he believes is *true*; and he's *justified* in believing what he does, that is, he doesn't get it right "just by accident" but for good and sufficient reasons. There's a long philosophical tradition that identifies knowledge with justified true belief in this way, and it seems plausible enough to me. Who am I to argue with long philosophical traditions?

EDIE: You don't have to be anyone special. You can argue with *any* traditions, long or short, as long as you make your case. All that counts is the quality of your reasoning. But let me make sure I understand your position. The true belief part is straightforward enough, but I'm not so clear about being justified. When you say that he gets it right, not by accident, but for good and sufficient reasons, do you mean that *there are* some good reasons that *account* for his getting it right or that *he has* some good reasons for getting it right?

JUSTIN: I mean that there has to be a good answer to the question "How does he know it?"

EDIE: That doesn't answer my question. What I want to know is whether it's enough that there be *some explanation or other* of why he believes that K or whether that explanation has to have a certain form, one which gives *his* reasons for regarding himself as *entitled* to believe it.

JUSTIN: I'm not sure I see the difference.

EDIE: Well, maybe it is a little slippery. The problem is that it makes sense to talk about "reasons" wherever there's any kind of '*because*'. We "give reasons" whenever we offer an explanation of anything, but the point is that there are different kinds of explanations and so different kinds of 'because's as well.

One kind occurs in causal explanations. A causal explanation explains why, given that one thing happened in certain circumstances, another thing then *had to* happen; why a certain thing's subsequently happening was inevitable in those circumstances. For instance: "Why did the six-ball roll into the pocket? Because it was firmly struck by the cue ball at such-and-such an angle." In this sense, a person might believe that K because he's been *brainwashed* into believing it. That would account for the fact that he believes it, but it's entirely noncommittal about whether K is a reasonable thing for him or anyone to believe.

But another sort of 'because' occurs in what are sometimes called 'rationalizations'. A person offers a rationalization when explains why *by his lights* it is or was reasonable to do something or to believe something, why one *ought to* do or believe a certain thing in certain circumstances. "Why did I target the six-ball? Because I'd just sunk the five-ball, and I have to sink them in numerical sequence in order to win." In this sense, a person might believe that K because he's concluded that K follows from other things that he knows and believes. Of course, not all rationalizations are successful. There are bad reasons as well as good reasons for doing and believing things. But a successful rationalization, that is, one which cites sufficiently good reasons, can not only account for the fact that someone believes something but can at the same time also explain why he's entitled to believe what he does.

JUSTIN: I *think* that what's needed for knowledge are the 'rationalization' kind of good reasons, but I'm still not sure that I've really nailed down the distinction you have in mind. Can you try it one more time?

EDIE: Maybe this will help. Do you think that animals know things? I mean animals like dogs and cats and squirrels, not animals like us.

JUSTIN: I guess so. At least some animals do. I had a dog once who seemed to know when I was going to take her out for a walk. Whenever I'd get out her leash, she'd run over to the door, scratch on it a couple of times, and sit there waiting. So I guess she knew that the leash meant it was time for her to go out.

EDIE: OK, you say that your dog knew when you were going to take her out for a walk. According to your account of knowing, that means that, on certain occasions, your dog believed that she was going out for a walk, and her belief was true, and she was justified in believing it. She wasn't right just by accident, but for good reasons. My question is: What sort of reasons? Why did your dog believe that she was going for a walk?

JUSTIN: She saw me take out her leash.

EDIE: So your dog reasoned: "Justin's getting out the leash, so it must be time for a walk"?

JUSTIN: Well, I don't think she actually engaged in any *reasoning*. She'd just learned to associate the two things. It was like a conditioned response. The one thing had been followed by the other often enough so that when she saw me take out the leash, she expected to go for a walk. The sight of the leash automatically triggered the belief.

EDIE: That's a causal explanation, then. Your dog's true belief was caused by the sight of the leash. It's not a rationalization.

JUSTIN: That seems right. I think that what you're calling rationalizations only apply to people who can say what their reasons are and debate about whether they're good or bad reasons.

EDIE: So, if animals can know things, and knowing implies being justified, then being justified *doesn't* imply being able to give and evaluate reasons, but only that there's some explanation—for instance, a causal one—of why a particular individual has a true belief on a particular occasion.

SKIP: Whether or not you agree with Gemma about what *people* know, I think it's confused to say that animals know things in the first place. I don't even see how you can say that your dog *believed* anything. I know that people like to talk about their pets as if they were people, but they're not! That's just anthropomorphizing.

JUSTIN: If she didn't believe that she was going for a walk, why did my dog go over and wait by the door?

SKIP: You've already given the explanation. It was a conditioned response, like Pavlov's dog salivating whenever Pavlov rang a bell. Salivating isn't believing anything, and neither is scratching at a door. What do you gain by talking about your dog's belief? You say that the sight of the leash automatically triggered a belief, but why not just say that it automatically triggered the *behavior*?

JUSTIN: Well, I suppose that you could look at it that way. But don't we normally interpret behavior as indicating or expressing certain beliefs?

EDIE: I think you *should* look at it that way, Justin. Of course we interpret *people's* behavior as indicating or expressing their beliefs, but it's legitimate to do that only because there's something that counts as getting it right or wrong, as interpreting it correctly or incorrectly. People can *tell us* what they believe. Dogs can't do that. In the case of your dog, the only thing there is to go on is the behavior. The whole point of talking about someone's beliefs, however, is to connect his behavior with particular rationalizations. If a person is carrying an umbrella, it might be because he believes that it's going to rain, but it might also be because he believes that it makes him look distinguished, or that it might come in handy for self-defense, or that it keeps evil demons away, or for any of a million other reasons. That's the point. People have reasons for behaving in the ways they do. The way that dogs and other animals behave, in contrast, is either instinctive or conditioned. Reasons don't enter into it.

GEMMA: *Of course* dogs believe things! And they do things for reasons, too.

SKIP: Obviously I agree with Edie at this point.

JUSTIN: Frankly, I'm not really sure what I want to say. I said that my dog *seemed* to know when I was going to take her for a walk, but that might just be a convenient way of talking, since I don't think that we can literally explain animals' behavior in the rationalizing way. But we don't actually have to decide about animals, do we? If I've understood Edie correctly, the example of animals was originally brought up only to illustrate her distinction between causal and rationalizing explanations. Her *question* was which sort of explanation I thought was required in order for a true belief to be justified, and that question still makes sense in the case of people, whatever we might decide to say about animals. I'm not really sure what I want to say about that, either, but I'm prepared to try out the simpler answer, that a person's true belief is justified, and so counts as knowledge, if there's *any* sort of good explanation of why he's got it right. Won't that do?

EDIE: I don't think so. Let's try another example. Suppose we discover someone who's usually right about which direction she's facing. Call her Nora. It doesn't make any difference where Nora happens to be—in a city, in a desert, or in a jungle; on the road, at sea, or in an airplane—if you ask her which way she thinks she's facing, and then check her answer by using a reliable compass, most of the time she turns out to be right. In other words, Nora is someone who finds herself with mostly true beliefs about the directions she's facing at various times, the same way that we find ourselves with mostly true beliefs about, for example, the colors of things in our vicinity at various times.

Let's suppose that the *explanation* of these facts about Nora is that, unbeknownst to her, she is the subject of a unique experiment. A group of bionic engineers have implanted a small electronic compass under her skin and wired it into her brain in just the way necessary to induce such beliefs. Now according to your "simpler answer," Justin, we should say that Nora *knows* which way she's facing at any given time, since there is a good explanation of why she has a correct belief about the direction in which she's facing when she does. But I don't think she does know.

JUSTIN: Why not?

EDIE: Because she has no reason to think that her beliefs *are* correct. *We* have a reason to trust Nora's beliefs about which way she's facing. We've independently checked them out and discovered that they're reliable. But as far as the story goes, *Nora* doesn't have any reason to trust her beliefs about such things. When the question of which way she's facing arises, she just finds herself with a suitable belief. We know that it's also likely to be a true belief and even why it's likely to be correct, but Nora doesn't know any of that. For all she knows, she's just guessing.

JUSTIN: But that doesn't show that Nora doesn't know which way she's facing. It only shows that Nora doesn't *know that* she knows it. If she's facing north, for example, she's still justified in believing that she's facing north even if she doesn't know that she's justified in believing it.

EDIE: Suppose we asked Nora why she believes that she's facing north. She'd have no answer.

GEMMA: What's wrong with that? There are lots of things that we *just* believe, aren't there?

EDIE: Perhaps there are. But the question is whether something that someone *just* believes can be something that she knows, something that she's justified in believing. My view is that someone is justified in believing only what she's *entitled* to believe, and that Nora isn't entitled to believe that she's facing north on a given occasion until she herself knows that her spontaneous beliefs of that sort are generally reliable. That doesn't mean that she needs to know about the implanted compass and all that. After all, we don't need to know about all that in order to know that she's reliable about directions. All we need to know is her track record, that is, that her beliefs about which direction she's facing are usually correct. But if Nora doesn't even know *that* about herself, then, from her perspective, her present belief that she's facing north is just a *hunch*, and if she's responsible about beliefs and good reasons, she'd have to confess herself that she's not entitled to place any confidence in it.

JUSTIN: That still doesn't show that she doesn't know it. What she doesn't know is that she's entitled to trust her spontaneous beliefs about directions. But, whether she knows it or not, she *is* entitled to trust them.

EDIE: I don't think so. After all, Nora also knows that people's hunches about which directions they're facing are usually *un*reliable. Given her ignorance both of the implanted compass and even of her own track record, then, she should conclude that she's *not* entitled to trust her own spontaneous beliefs about directions. And surely that's correct. There's nothing wrong with her reasoning, is there?

JUSTIN: Yes there is. It has a false premise. Nora's assuming that she's just like everybody else—but she's not. Other people don't have electronic compasses implanted under their skin and wired into their brains.

EDIE: Of course not. But she doesn't know about that. For all she knows, she *is* just like everybody else. That's all she's entitled to believe. And the only conclusions she's entitled to accept are those that follow from premises that she's entitled to believe.

JUSTIN: I think we're just destined to disagree about Nora. I still don't see how her spontaneous beliefs about directions are different from my own spontaneous beliefs about colors. Her beliefs about the direction she's facing are mostly correct, and so are my beliefs about the colors of objects in my vicinity. So Nora knows that she's facing north because that's how it *feels* to her, and I know that Skip's wearing a blue T-shirt because that's how it *looks* to me. The only difference is that I was born with reliable color-detecting organs, and Nora got hers from some bionic engineering.

EDIE: That's not the only difference. You know that you're generally reliable about colors, that you're not color-blind, for example. And you also know in what sorts of circumstances you're likely to make mistakes, for instance, when you're wearing sunglasses or the lighting isn't normal. So you're in a position to reason: "It looks like Skip's wearing a blue T-shirt; there's nothing special or peculiar about the circumstances; so it's reasonable for me to believe that Skip *is* wearing a blue T-shirt."

JUSTIN: Do you mean that you have to reason like that in order to know that Skip's T-shirt is blue? Because people don't.

EDIE: No, of course they don't. But they *could*. My view is that you have to *be in a position* to reason like that in order to know it. You have to know that you're generally reliable about colors and at least not have any reason to believe that there's anything abnormal about the circumstances.

SKIP: Are you saying that that's good enough for knowing?

EDIE: I think so. At least, I'm inclined to agree with Justin about what it takes for knowing—justified true belief, but not certainty. Our disagreement isn't about that, but about what it takes for a belief to be justified.

SKIP: Well, what about a case like this: It's a bright sunny day; I'm out in the country; and it looks to me like there's a sheep in a certain meadow. Let's suppose that I'm generally reliable about sheep. I know a sheep when I see one. I don't confuse them with cows or goats, for example. So I believe that there's a sheep in the meadow. And let's suppose that there *is* a sheep in the meadow, so that my belief is true. I'm even in a position to reason "It looks like there's a sheep in the meadow; there's nothing special or peculiar about the circumstances; so it's reasonable for me to believe that there's a sheep in the meadow." So I have a justified true belief that there's a sheep in the meadow. Do I *know* that there's a sheep in the meadow?

EDIE: Why wouldn't you know it?

SKIP: Because what I'm actually looking at is a rock that, from where I'm standing, looks *just like* a sheep. It doesn't just look that way because there's something special about me. It would look just like a sheep to anyone who was standing there. There actually *is* a sheep in the meadow, but it's behind the rock, and I can't see it from where I am. So my belief is true. I do get it right. But even though I'm justified in believing what I do, I get it right "by accident".

JUSTIN: Wait a minute! If you get it right by accident, then you're *not* justified in believing what you do.

SKIP: What more do I need? You've already said that you know that I'm wearing a blue T-shirt because that's how it looks to you; your beliefs about the colors of things in your vicinity are mostly correct; and this one actually *is* correct. Well, it looks to me as if there's a sheep in the meadow; my beliefs about the presence of sheep in my vicinity are mostly correct; and this one actually *is* correct. So on your account I *do* know that there's a sheep in the meadow, don't I?

JUSTIN: No, if you got it right by accident, then you don't know it. That's not something I'm willing to give up. The proper conclusion is surely that it takes more for a belief to be justified than we've talked about so far.

SKIP: That's what I've been saying all along! If justification is going to suffice for knowing, what it takes is certainty. You have to be able to rule out the possibility of being mistaken.

JUSTIN: I still think that's too strong. I do know that you're wearing a blue shirt, even though I can't absolutely rule out every remotely conceivable way in which my belief that you are might be mistaken, Martians manipulating my mind, for instance, or something equally fantastic. But your sheep example shows that it takes something more for a belief to be justified than for it to be reasonable to believe it given the way things look in the circumstances. Given the way things look to you from where you're standing, it *is* reasonable for you to believe that there's a sheep in the meadow. So what's the difference? I think it's in the *causes* of the two beliefs. In your story, your belief that there's a sheep in the meadow is caused by a rock that looks like a sheep, but my belief that you're wearing a blue shirt is caused by the fact that you're wearing a blue shirt.

SKIP: So what you're proposing is that in order for a belief to be justified, it not only needs to be reasonable to believe it in the given circumstances, it also needs to be caused in a certain way?

JUSTIN: That's right. It needs to be caused by the very fact that it's about. You don't know that the sheep is in the meadow unless you can see it, and you don't see it unless your visual experience is caused in the usual way, by light reflected from the sheep entering your eyes and stimulating the rods and cones or whatever.

EDIE: That sounds like a sensible proposal. Being caused in the right way is necessary for remembering, too, and that's how we know various things about the past. If someone seems to remember doing something when he was four years old, say, tipping over a menorah, only because he's been told the story of how he did it so many times, then he doesn't actually remember it. His memory experience has to be caused by the actual event itself.

GEMMA: Are you saying that someone can't know that he did something when he was four unless he remembers it himself? That doesn't sound right. Lots of what I know about what I did when I was very little I know because my parents and grandparents told me about it.

EDIE: No, I'm not saying that a person can only know about what he remembers himself. Hearing the testimony of other people is a perfectly good way of coming to know something, provided that it's honest and reliable testimony. That's why we cross-examine eyewitnesses in court, for example. Once it's established that their testimony is trustworthy, the jury can rely on it in coming to know what happened. But remembering something oneself is *one* way of knowing it, and what I'm saying is that a memory experience needs to be caused in the right way in order to count as actually remembering, just like a visual experience of something needs to be caused in the right way in order to count as actually seeing it.

SKIP: So you and Justin now agree that, in order for a true belief to count as knowledge, it needs to be justified in the sense of *both* being reasonable to believe in the circumstances *and* being caused in the normal way. Is that also supposed to be *sufficient* for it to count as something known?

JUSTIN: I'd say so, except that it sounds like you have another story up your sleeve.

SKIP: How well you know me! I do indeed. It's a story about someone I'll call 'Sam'. Sam lives on Wayout Island, 30 miles off the coast. Wayout Island is served by a mail boat that's scheduled to stop there every weekday afternoon at 3 P.M., and, as everyone who lives on the island knows, the mail service is generally quite reliable. The mail boat almost always arrives at just about 3 o'clock, although it has, of course, occasionally been unavoidably delayed by mechanical troubles, rough seas, or the like. Other boats, for instance, private motor yachts and fishing boats, also come and go at Wayout Island fairly frequently, but at various times of day, not on such a regular schedule.

One clear and sunny Tuesday afternoon, Sam is standing on the wharf and looking out to sea. At 2:50 P.M., noting a speck that has just appeared on the distant horizon, he judges that it is the mail boat, arriving on time. "There's the mail boat," he thinks to himself. That's what he believes, and, as it subsequently turns out, he's right. The speck that he saw on the distant horizon was the mail boat.

Now as far as I can tell, you'd have to say that Sam *knew* that the speck on the horizon was the mail boat. It was certainly reasonable for him to believe that. The mail boat was due at 3 o'clock, and, like everybody else, he knew that the boat was very reliable. It almost always arrived on schedule. And his belief was caused in the right way. He *saw* the mail boat on the distant horizon. What stimulated his eyes and produced his belief was light reflected from it. So according to you, Sam's true belief was also appropriately justified. Sam had a justified true belief, and so he knew that the speck on the horizon was the mail boat. But it's obvious that he *didn't* know that at all. For all he knew, this might have been one of those times that the mail boat was late, and the speck on the horizon could just as well have been one of those private yachts or fishing boats that also frequently visit Wayout Island.

JUSTIN: I'm not sure it is obvious that he doesn't know it. I agree that Sam can't rule out the possibility that what he sees on the horizon is a private yacht or fishing boat rather than the mail boat. The mail boat might have been delayed. But there's no reason for Sam to believe that the mail boat *was* delayed. The reasonable thing for him to believe is still that what he sees *is* the mail boat, and that belief is also true and caused in the right way. Sure, it was possible for him to be mistaken, but, remember, I don't agree that you can know something only if you can rule out every possibility for being mistaken. I reject the view that knowing requires being certain.

EDIE: I don't know, Justin. Skip's story convinced me. I agree with you that Sam doesn't have to be able to rule out *every* possibility for being mistaken—I don't think he needs to be *certain* that it's the mail boat that he sees—but I think he has to be able to rule out *some* of them, the realistic ones at least, and that includes the possibilities that Skip mentioned. It's not enough that he be able to see the mail boat. He doesn't know that it's the mail boat until he's entitled to be confident that it is, and that isn't true unless he can see *that it is* the mail boat. But he can't do that while it's still a speck on the distant horizon. All boats look alike at that distance. It's reasonable for him to *expect* the mail boat at 3 o'clock, and so it's reasonable for him to believe that what he sees is the mail boat, but he doesn't know that it is until he gets a better look at it. Just seeing it isn't good enough. He needs to be able to *recognize* it.

GEMMA: I think Edie's right, too. You don't have to be able to rule out every possibility for being mistaken, only the realistic ones. But once Sam's done that, then he *is* certain that what he sees is the mail boat. Once he can see what's approaching the island clearly enough to recognize that it *is* the mail boat and rule out the possibility that it's one of those yachts or fishing boats, then he has absolutely no reason to doubt that the mail boat is what he sees. He not only knows that it is; he's certain that it is.

SKIP: Well, it looks like we could hardly disagree more. I've suggested that Sam can't know that the speck he sees on the horizon is the mail boat because he can't rule out every possibility for being mistaken. Justin, in contrast, thinks that Sam *does* know that what he sees is the mail boat, even though he can't rule out the possibility that it's a private yacht or fishing boat. Edie agrees with me that Sam doesn't know it's the mail boat when it's just a speck on the horizon, but she thinks that he *does* know it once he gets a good enough look at it to recognize it as the mail boat, even if he can't ever be absolutely certain. And Gemma agrees with Edie, except that she thinks that once Sam gets a good enough look at the mail boat, he not only can be, but actually *is* absolutely certain that that's what he sees.

JUSTIN: So where do we go from here?

EDIE: Well, where *I* go is to my afternoon classes, I'm afraid. As much as I'm enjoying this, I do have some obligations.

JUSTIN: But you'd be willing to carry on?

EDIE: Oh, more than just willing. Eager. We just need to find another good time and place to get together. How about after dinner tonight in the Café Coffee?

GEMMA: I'm busy tonight—and besides, I need more time to think about all this than just one afternoon. How about after dinner tomorrow?

EDIE: I can make it then.

JUSTIN: Sounds good to me, too. Skip?

SKIP: Seven thirty tomorrow at the Café Caffeine it is. See you all there.

THE THIRD CONVERSATION

(In the Café Coffee the following evening. SKIP, GEMMA, EDIE, and JUSTIN have all bought drinks and made themselves comfortable at a table in the corner.)

SKIP: I've got another story.

EDIE: Will it help us decide which of us is right about Sam and the mail boat?

SKIP: I don't know. But it does show that what we should say about Sam doesn't depend on the fact that the boat he sees on the horizon is too far away for him to recognize what sort of boat it is.

JUSTIN: Let's hear it.

SKIP: OK. It starts with something that happened when they were making the film *The Barns of Madison County*. It was actually filmed in Madison County, you know. There are plenty of genuine barns there, but the producer decided that there weren't enough, and so he added a few fake barn sets. They looked just like barns from the road, but they were only facades.

GEMMA: Like Potemkin villages!

SKIP: What are they?

GEMMA: The same sort of thing. Fake villages, designed to look real from a passing coach or train. Potemkin was Catherine the Great's prime minister near the end of the eighteenth century. He constructed the fake villages so that she'd think that Russia was prospering when she traveled through it.

SKIP: OK. So the film crew built some Potemkin barns. It should be obvious how the rest of the story goes. One

sunny day, someone—I'll call him George—is driving
through Madison County. He looks out the window
of his car, and he sees what looks like a barn. "There's
a handsome barn," he thinks. He has a clear, unob-
structed view of it, and he knows what a barn looks
like. He doesn't confuse barns with other sorts of
buildings. So it's entirely reasonable for George to
believe that there's a barn over there. And he's right.
What he sees *is* a nice-looking barn. So his belief is
also caused in the normal way. According to Justin,
then, his belief is not only true but also justified, and
he'd have to say that George knows that what he's
looking at is a barn. But it seems obvious that George
doesn't know that it is. For all he knows, it might be
one of those Potemkin barns.

EDIE: Nice example, Skip. The problem obviously isn't that
George doesn't get a good enough look at the barn.
It's right there in plain view. The problem is that he
can't discriminate real barns from fake barns just by
looking.

JUSTIN: Nevertheless, I'm going to say the same thing about
George and the barn that I said about Sam and the
mail boat. There's no reason for him to believe that
what he sees is just a facade. The reasonable thing for
him to believe is that he's looking at a barn, and that
belief is both true and caused in the normal way. So
he does know that there's a barn over there. .

EDIE: I don't think it's that simple, Justin. For instance, suppose that George *knows* that he's driving through
Madison County. Then he'll know that not everything
that looks like a barn is one, and so he's not entitled
to be completely confident that what he sees is a barn.
Now, is it still reasonable for him to believe that it is?
I think that depends on how many Potemkin barns
there are. If there are just as many fake barns as there
are real ones, for example, he won't know what to
believe. It'll be just as reasonable for him to believe
that what he's seeing is a Potemkin barn as that it's a
real one.

JUSTIN: Well, I was assuming that there are just a few fake barns and lots of real ones.

EDIE: I don't think that makes a difference. In fact, isn't this really just like the lottery case? Whenever anyone drives through Madison County, he's automatically entered in the Potemkin barn lottery. Even if there's only one of them, since it looks just like all the genuine barns, although it may be highly improbable that it's the one George happens to be looking at, and entirely reasonable for him to believe that it's a real barn, there's still some chance that his number has come up in the Potemkin barn lottery and that he's mistaken. So George doesn't know that what he's looking at is a real barn.

JUSTIN: That's a tough call. But if it *is* like the lottery case, then it's the random factor that prevents George from knowing. It may be reasonable for him to believe that it's a real barn, but he's not *justified* in believing it.

SKIP: But then its being reasonable to believe something and the belief's being caused in the right way aren't sufficient for the belief to be justified. You're going to have to build in something else, to rule out Potemkin barn type cases. May I suggest that what you need is the requirement that George must be absolutely certain that what he sees is a real barn?

JUSTIN: You can suggest it all you want, but I'm not going to accept your suggestion. I still think that there are lots of ways of being justified in believing something that stop well short of certainty. Basically, it's a matter of having good enough evidence or reasons for what you believe. Sometimes just the way something looks to you can be a good enough reason. That's how I know you're still wearing that blue T-shirt.

SKIP: It's a *different* blue T-shirt.

JUSTIN: Whatever. But what your Potemkin barn story shows is that sometimes you need more than just the way something looks. I'm not sure that there's any simple, general way of explaining when you have good enough evidence or reasons for a true belief to count as knowing, though.

EDIE: Actually, I think there are some real problems with the notion of justification. For instance, what makes something a reason for believing something else? Let's say that what you believe is that K. What *counts* as a reason for believing that K?

JUSTIN: How about evidence that K is true?

EDIE: But what makes something evidence for the truth of K? Suppose that you discover that something else is true, say, E. How does the truth of E have to be related to the truth of K in order to count as *evidence* that K is also true?

JUSTIN: Well, if the truth of K *follows from* the truth of E, that is, if it would be self-contradictory to suppose that E is true but K isn't, then E is certainly evidence that K is true. Conclusive evidence, in fact.

EDIE: But not all evidence is conclusive evidence, is it?

JUSTIN: No. Some evidence just makes what it's evidence for more probable. I'd say that, in general, E is evidence for K if the fact that E is true makes it *more likely* that K is true. Conclusive evidence is a special case of that. Think of a scientist testing an hypothesis. On the basis of her hypothesis, she predicts how certain experiments should turn out, and then she performs those experiments. The fact that a given experiment actually yields the predicted result counts as evidence in favor of her hypothesis, since the more such predictions turn out to be correct, the more likely it is that her hypothesis is true.

EDIE: All right. That seems clear enough. Now you say that someone is justified in believing that K just in case he has good enough evidence or reasons, E, for believing it. Would it amount to the same thing to say that someone's belief that K is justified if he believes it *on the basis of* good enough evidence or reasons, E?

JUSTIN: That sounds OK. Is it going to get me into any trouble?

EDIE: That depends. I'd say that believing one thing *on the basis of* another suggests a rationalizing explanation. That is, the picture I get is of justification being *transmitted* from one belief to another by reasoning. So, in order for me to be justified in believing K on the basis of E, I need to be justified in believing E. But then, if being justified is always a matter of having good enough evidence or reasons for what one believes, I can be justified in believing E only if I believe it on the basis of *further* evidence or reasons, say, F, and then I'll need to be justified in believing F, and so on. In other words, the notion of justification as having good enough reasons or evidence seems to lead to an infinite regress.

GEMMA: Not necessarily. The chain of reasons and evidence doesn't have to be infinite. It could ultimately lead back to K.

JUSTIN: But then you'd have no justification at all! If A is supposed to be justified on the basis of B, and B on the basis of C, and C on the basis of D, and D on the basis of A again, then we just go around in a circle. The whole thing just floats in the air, and nothing ever actually gets justified.

GEMMA: Why couldn't the justification result from the coherence of the whole *system* of beliefs? What justifies any *individual* belief would be the fact that it belongs to a consistent and coherent system of mutually supporting beliefs.

JUSTIN: But there can be lots of different coherent systems of beliefs, systems whose individual beliefs would sometimes contradict one another. They couldn't *all* be justified.

GEMMA: Well, I agree that a pair of contradictory beliefs couldn't both be justified, but I'm not sure that I accept your other premise, the one about the possibility of lots of different coherent systems. It seems to be a hard enough job just keeping *one* system of beliefs mutually consistent and coherent.

JUSTIN: The fact remains that, in order for there to be any justification, the whole system of beliefs has to somehow be *anchored*. Otherwise one belief couldn't *support* another. Not all justification can be transmitted from beliefs to other beliefs. There has to be some *original source* of justification. Some beliefs have to be justified, not indirectly or derivatively, on the basis of other beliefs, but directly and immediately, by the world, for instance, by the fact that they've been caused in the right way.

EDIE: But surely what the examples of Sam and the mail boat and George and the Potemkin barns show is that the mere fact that a belief has been caused in a particular way isn't sufficient by itself to justify believing it. It also has to be something that it's *reasonable* to believe. Of course, if by "caused in the *right* way" you mean "caused in a way that makes it likely that the belief is true," then being caused in the right way will normally be sufficient for justification. But that just amounts to saying that it would be correct to argue: "This belief—call it 'B'—was caused in such and such a way; in normal circumstances, beliefs caused in that way are likely to be true; there's no reason to believe that the present circumstances aren't normal; so it's likely to be true that B; so it's reasonable to believe that B." I think that whether or not a given belief is justified *always* depends upon whether other beliefs are justified. Your being justified in believing that Skip is still wearing a blue T-shirt depends, for instance, on your being justified in believing that there's nothing odd about the lighting, that you haven't suddenly become colorblind, and so on.

JUSTIN: No. It just depends on those things being *true*. I don't need to believe them.

SKIP: I think you're right about an original source of justification, Justin. If you know anything, then there have to be some true beliefs that you're justified in holding, but not on the basis of other beliefs. Let's call them *basic* beliefs. But I agree with Edie that the mere fact that a belief was caused in this or that way can't be enough to make it a basic belief. That's because there's *more* to being a basic belief than just being non-derivatively justified and true. You also have to be able to appeal to it to justify *other* beliefs. So you not only have to be justified in holding it, you have to *know* that you're justified in holding it. Otherwise you wouldn't be justified in *using* it as a reason for believing anything else.

JUSTIN: So how would you end Edie's regress?

SKIP: In the obvious way—with *self-justifying* beliefs.

JUSTIN: How in the world can a belief be self-justifying?

SKIP: By being a belief that you can't be mistaken about! The mere fact that you believe it is enough to guarantee that it's true. What Descartes discovered is that there are indeed self-justifying beliefs, but none of them are beliefs about the world. His own example was "*Cogito; ergo, sum*", "I think; therefore, I exist". If you believe that you're thinking, then you *are* thinking, and the mere fact that you believe that you exist—or believe anything else, for that matter— implies that you *do* exist.

JUSTIN: Isn't that a belief about the world?

SKIP: Not about the *external* world, the world of things that you seem to perceive through the senses. You can be mistaken about any of them, including your own body. You might just be a brain in a vat. There are other beliefs that can't be mistaken, but they're not about the world either. They're all about how things *seem*. Your belief that I'm wearing a blue shirt can be mistaken, but not your belief that it *seems to you* that I am.

JUSTIN: So basic beliefs have to be beliefs that you can't be mistaken about. Back to certainty again!

SKIP: I never left it.

JUSTIN: But if none of our basic beliefs are about the world, then how can they be evidence or reasons for believing anything about the world?

EDIE: We need to put them together with other things we know. It seems to you that Skip is wearing a blue shirt. Maybe you can't be mistaken about that, and maybe you can. I don't want to commit myself about that. But if you're normally a reliable reporter of the colors of things in your vicinity and there's nothing abnormal about your present circumstances, then the fact that it seems to you that Skip is wearing a blue shirt *is* evidence that he's wearing one. That's the most likely explanation of why it seems to you that he is.

JUSTIN: Well, *I* think that's OK, but Skip won't. I do believe that I'm a reliable color-reporter and that there's nothing unusual about my present circumstances, but those aren't *basic* beliefs. They're beliefs about the world, and I could obviously be mistaken about them. Unbeknownst to me, I might have suddenly become colorblind, or they might recently have installed peculiar lighting in here. So Skip will surely conclude that I can't use basic beliefs as evidence for the truth of other beliefs about the world, for instance, the color of his shirt, unless I can first show that *those* beliefs about the world are true using only basic beliefs as evidence. And I don't see how that's possible.

SKIP: Neither do I—and that's why I claim that we *don't* know anything about the world. Descartes thought it was possible, but that's only because he thought some of his basic beliefs provided conclusive evidence of the existence of God—and, as you can imagine, there's *lots* of disagreement about his very odd argument for that conclusion.

GEMMA: If basic beliefs are ones you can't be mistaken about, then there *are* basic beliefs about the world. You couldn't be mistaken about there being many people and objects in the world, for example. There are lots of beliefs like that, beliefs that we know for certain are true, and any of them can be part of our evidence or reasons for believing other things about the world.

SKIP: But you *could* be mistaken about that!

GEMMA: If *you're* telling *me* that I could be mistaken about something, then there are at least two people in the world. Neither of us could be mistaken about that, could we?

JUSTIN: I think all this worrying about certainty is just a red herring. I agree with Skip that there have to be *some* basic beliefs. But even if they are all just about how things seem to me, I agree with Edie that I can still use them as evidence for the truth of other beliefs about the world, because *not all* our reasons or evidence have to be certain. I can start by assuming that I'm a reliable color-reporter in normal circumstances, and justify my beliefs about what colors things are by appealing to my basic beliefs about what colors they seem to me to be. Then I can check those beliefs against other people's beliefs about the colors of things. If we disagree, then I might have to give up my assumption that I'm a reliable color-reporter or that these are normal circumstances, or that the people whom I asked are themselves reliable about colors, or some other assumption. As long as I don't need to arrive at absolute certainty, there's nothing that prevents me from ultimately being justified in believing that Skip is wearing a blue T-shirt, that is, having reasons and evidence for believing it that are sufficient for me to know it, if it's also true.

GEMMA: That sounds a lot like my "coherent system of beliefs" proposal that you didn't like earlier.

JUSTIN: I don't think it's the same thing. My story has *basic* beliefs in it, for example.

EDIE: I still think that there are serious problems about the notion of justification all by itself, even without worrying about basic beliefs and coherent systems. Justin, am I right to assume that a belief's being justified is one thing and its being true is something else? I mean, there can be true beliefs that aren't justified—lucky guesses, for example—but also justified beliefs that aren't true, that is, justified false beliefs, right? Skip might not agree, but you want to explain knowing in terms of justified true beliefs, and that suggests that you think we need two *different* things for knowing, justification and truth.

JUSTIN: I hadn't really thought about it, but you're obviously right. If I reject Skip's view that knowing requires being absolutely certain, then being a justified true belief will be consistent with the possibility of being mistaken, and being justified will consequently be consistent with *actually* being mistaken. So there can be justified false beliefs.

EDIE: And is it safe to assume that justification is transmitted over logical implication? I mean, if I'm justified in believing one thing, say, that Skip's shirt is blue, and I know that something else *follows from* what I believe, for instance, that Skip's shirt is colored, and I draw that conclusion and come to believe the second thing, then I'm justified in believing it too, right?

JUSTIN: Obviously. Being justified is just having good enough evidence or reasons for believing what you do. If certain facts make it likely that some belief is true, then they also make it at least as likely that whatever follows from that belief is true. So if you're justified in believing that something is true, then you're also justified in believing all the things that are implied by its being true.

EDIE: OK. My turn to tell a story. Suppose that I believe that Bruce got an A in sociology, and that I'm justified in believing it. For instance, Bruce might so far have a straight-A average in his other courses, and I might also know that he got A's on his first two sociology papers and on the midterm exam. Now if Bruce got an A in sociology, it follows that *someone* got an A, and so I'm also justified in believing that. Finally, suppose that someone *did* get an A in sociology—my belief that someone did is not only justified, but also true—but that, as it happens, it wasn't Bruce. It was Betty, about whom I know nothing at all. Unbeknownst to me, Bruce self-destructed on the final exam. So I believe that someone got an A, and I'm justified in believing it, and my belief is true. But would you say that I *know* that someone got an A in sociology? I wouldn't. I got it right by accident.

JUSTIN: That's kind of like the case of the rock and the sheep. If we assumed that I was justified in believing that *the thing I see* in the meadow is a sheep, because it looks just like a sheep, then, since that implies that *there is* a sheep in the meadow, I'd be justified in believing that, too. We're supposing that it's true that there is a sheep in the meadow, so I would have a justified true belief, but one that didn't count as knowing. That's another good reason for saying that I'm not justified in believing that the thing I see is a sheep, that being justified requires that the belief be caused in the right way.

EDIE: But the problem doesn't depend on what it takes to be justified, as long as there can still be justified false beliefs. If you have any two beliefs, X and Y, such that Y follows from X and your belief that X is justified, then, *whatever* it takes to be justified, your belief that Y will also be justified. If Y is also true, then you'll have a justified true belief. But if the *only* reason that you have for believing Y is that you've inferred it from X and X happens to be false, then your justified true belief that Y won't count as knowing. You'll have gotten it right only by accident. So, *whatever* it takes to be justified, there has to be more to knowing than having a justified true belief. That's the problem. What else does it take?

JUSTIN: Well, why not just require that the reasoning you use to arrive at your justified *true* belief mustn't use any *false* beliefs as premises? That ought to do it.

EDIE: I thought that would work, too. It does take care of my belief that someone got an A in sociology. But then I came up with another example. This one's kind of weird.

SKIP: I love weird stories!

EDIE: You should. You tell enough of them yourself. But I think this one's weirder than most of yours.

GEMMA: Don't keep us in suspense. How does it go?

EDIE: OK. I walk into a room, and there I see Otto's head. (I told you it was weird!) "Omigod!", I think, "Otto's been decapitated." And then the realization hits me: "Otto's been murdered. So Otto's dead." Now not only is my belief that Otto is dead both justified and true, but I certainly think that I *know* that he's dead. But here's the catch: If we add the requirement that the reasoning I used to arrive at my justified true belief mustn't use any false beliefs as premises, then I *don't* know it. Because Otto *wasn't* murdered. He died of natural causes, and then, later, a mad fiend cut off his head. So my actual reasoning *did* use a false belief, the false belief that Otto was murdered.

GEMMA: That's not just a weird story. It's positively gruesome!

EDIE: Sorry about that.

JUSTIN: Never mind that. The question is, what does it tell us about knowing? It seems obvious that you *do* know that Otto is dead. And you did use a false premise . . . but you didn't have to! That's the solution! You could just as well have left it out and still had good enough reasons to justify your believing that Otto was dead. The reasoning then would have gone: "Otto's been decapitated; so Otto is dead." And that's good enough. After all, a person can't live without a head. So the reasoning didn't really *use* the false premise. Your true belief that Otto was dead already followed from your true belief that he'd been decapitated.

EDIE: So what would you add to justified true belief as the fourth requirement for knowing?

JUSTIN: Let's see. How about this: The reasoning that you use to arrive at your true belief mustn't make any *essential* use of false beliefs as premises.

EDIE: So if I have a justified true belief that I've arrived at by reasoning that uses only true premises, it'll count as knowing? Is that right?

JUSTIN: Now it sounds like you have *another* story.

EDIE: It must be habit-forming. I do indeed.

GEMMA: I hope it's not another gruesome one.

EDIE: No, it's very unexciting. It's about Everlight Matches. The Everlight Match company is very proud of their product. Everlights are manufactured to meet the highest industry standards and subjected to rigorous quality control. Consequently, they're extremely reliable. I personally, for example, have used hundreds of Everlights, and there hasn't been even one dud. Every single one of them has ignited when it was struck, and my friends and relatives have reported the same thing about the Everlight Matches that *they've* used. On the basis of all that evidence, I conclude that the next Everlight Match I take from the box I'm currently using will ignite when it is struck, and let us suppose that the evidence is quite sufficient for me to be justified in believing that. OK. So I open the box, take out a match, strike it, and—voilà!—it lights. My justified belief turned out to be true. I didn't make any use of false beliefs along the way. All my evidence was one hundred percent true. So according to the most recent proposal, I knew that the next Everlight Match out of the box would ignite when it was struck.

JUSTIN: And why didn't you?

EDIE: Because I got it right by accident. As it happens, that match was one of the tiny handful of defective ones ever to slip through the Everlight Match company's intensive quality control system. The only reason it ignited was that, just as I struck it, it was hit by a freak burst of cosmic rays.

SKIP: See? Nothing short of absolute certainty will do. You have to be able to rule out every possibility for being mistaken, including freak bursts of cosmic rays.

JUSTIN: Not so fast. Let me think about the example for a minute. I think I know where it goes wrong. You've described the case very carefully, Edie, but I think you left something out. I don't think that your belief was just that the next match would light when it was struck. I think that what someone in that situation would believe is that the next match would ignite when it was struck *because* it was struck. What all that evidence justifies you in believing, in other words, is that striking an Everlight Match *causes* it to light. So you did make tacit use of a false premise, the premise that striking the next match would *cause* it to ignite. You're not justified in believing that the match will light unless your beliefs about the causes are also true.

EDIE: I don't see why I have to grant that I have tacit beliefs about what causes matches to ignite at all, and, even if I do have them, I don't see why I should agree that I use them as "tacit premises". Why can't I just reason: "Striking an Everlight has been followed by its igniting thousands of times in the past. I know of no case in which an Everlight has been struck but has failed to light, so it's reasonable to believe that the next Everlight I strike will also ignite."

JUSTIN: Because the fact that one kind of event has been followed by another kind thousands of times in the past doesn't give you any reason at all to suppose that it will be followed by the other kind in the future unless you're tacitly assuming that there's some *connection* between the two sorts of events. Every time the storks come back to Sweden, the birth rate goes up, but there's no connection between those two events. It's just that they both occur about nine months after the start of a long, cold winter. We wouldn't expect more premature births if the storks happened to make it back a couple of months earlier one year. So the fact that striking an Everlight Match has regularly been followed by its lighting counts as a reason for believing that the next Everlight will ignite when struck only if it's interpreted as the fact that striking Everlight matches regularly *resulted in* their lighting, that is, that the striking is what caused the lighting.

GEMMA: That doesn't seem right to me. I think that we're generally justified in believing that the future will resemble the past—unless there's some good reason in a particular case for believing otherwise.

EDIE: That sounds like good topic for another day, but I don't think we need to go into it now. I'm ready to just *give* Justin his requirement that, in order for a justified true belief to count as knowing, the reasoning justifying it has to get the causes right, too. But that still isn't going to be sufficient, because I just realized that Skip's Potemkin barn case can satisfy all those requirements. When George sees what looks to him like a barn, he can reason: "That looks like a barn over there; in normal circumstances, I'm a highly reliable barn recognizer; I have no reason to believe that there's anything abnormal about these circumstances; so it's reasonable for me to believe that there is a barn over there." All George's premises are true, and so are his tacit beliefs about the causes. What he believes about causes is surely that his present experience is caused by a barn in the normal way, and we're assuming that it is. So George has a justified true belief, supported by reasoning that uses only true beliefs as premises, and he's also not mistaken about any causes. But he still doesn't know that there's a barn over there. Especially if there are lots of fake barns around, even though his belief that what he sees is a real barn is true, he gets it right only by accident.

JUSTIN: I haven't conceded that. Besides, the circumstances *are* abnormal—he's in Madison County, where there are fake barns—so there obviously *is* some reason to believe that they're abnormal. One of George's premises is false.

EDIE: I thought you did concede it—when we talked about the great Potemkin barn lottery. And George's premise *isn't* false. What he believes isn't that the circumstances *aren't* abnormal or even that there exists no reason to believe that they are. It's only that *he* has no reason to believe that the circumstances are abnormal, and that certainly can be true. All we need to suppose is that George doesn't know that he's in Madison County, or, even better, that he's never even heard of Madison County and the fake barns. For all he knows, everything that looks like a barn *is* a barn.

JUSTIN: Well, even if I do concede that George doesn't know that there's a barn over there, that's only because the random factor cancels out the possibility of knowing. If there are relatively few fake barns, then it may even be reasonable for him to believe that what he sees is a genuine barn, but he won't be *justified* in believing it.

EDIE: Why not? So far, all you've been requiring for someone's belief to be justified is that it's been caused in the normal way and it's reasonable for him to believe it on the basis of his evidence. George's belief that there's a barn over there satisfies those requirements, doesn't it? And that also seems to be a sensible and straightforward account of justification. The problem turned out to be that a true belief's being justified *in that sense* wasn't sufficient for it to count as knowing. So we added the requirements that the justified true belief must also have resulted from reasoning that made no essential use of false beliefs, including tacit false beliefs about causes, but the Potemkin barn case suggested that even *that* still wasn't sufficient to constitute knowing. So we obviously need to modify something. But rather than start fiddling with the notion of justification, why not just add *another* clause to the account of knowing?

JUSTIN: What other clause?

EDIE: Well, that's the question, isn't it? There's more to knowing than having a justified true belief, but, unless we buy into Skip's requirement of absolute certainty, there doesn't seem to be any straightforward way to say *what* more is needed, and Skip's story seems to imply that we've got to abandon the idea that we know anything about the world in the first place. I think we understand well enough what we want to rule out, cases in which someone is entirely justified in believing something that's true, but nevertheless has gotten it right only by accident. The problem is that there appear to be endless ways to get something right by accident. And that's only the beginning.

JUSTIN: What do you mean, only the beginning?

EDIE: I mean that we've mostly been talking only about one very simple *kind* of belief about the world, straightforward beliefs about objects in someone's immediate perceptual vicinity. But there are also beliefs about what *isn't* the case in the world, for example. George might also correctly believe, for instance, that there are no silos attached to the barn that he sees, but can he know that? What makes it reasonable for him to believe it? And what's the normal way for such a belief to be caused? By the absence of silos? And we've already mentioned *general* beliefs a couple of times, beliefs about what's always or usually the case. Can we ever know that any of them are true?

GEMMA: Sure we can. We can know all sorts of things about the world. And we not only *can* know things, we actually *do* know many things about the world. We shouldn't confuse the question of *whether* we know various things with the question of *how* we know them.

SKIP: But until we have an account of what knowing *is*, we don't know whether we know anything about the world.

GEMMA: No, that's backwards. One test of any account of knowing is that it doesn't imply that we can't know any of the innumerable things that we *do* know.

JUSTIN: I don't think that either Edie or I would quarrel with you about whether we know things about the world, Gemma. But you've got to remember that Skip didn't *just* deny that we know anything about the world. He had *reasons* for denying it. We got into all these puzzles by trying to figure out what to say about his arguments. I still think that what we need is an account of knowing in terms of some form of justified true belief that doesn't require absolute certainty, and I'm not yet convinced that we can't find one, but I do have to confess that I haven't yet figured out how to deal with all of Edie's worries.

EDIE: You haven't yet heard *all* of my worries about justification and knowing.

SKIP: And we're not going to hear them tonight. Look at the time.

GEMMA: Good grief! It's almost midnight! I don't know about you, but I've still got to do some reading for tomorrow. I've got a quiz in chemistry. Good night, all.

SKIP: 'Night, Gemma. Oh, one quick piece of advice about that quiz before you go.

GEMMA: What is it?

SKIP: Show 'em what you know!

(With laughter all around, the group breaks up and heads off to their rooms.)

REFERENCES

The First Conversation

SKIP is the epistemological *skeptic* in these conversations, defending the thesis that knowledge requires a form of absolute certainty and that, consequently, strictly speaking, we know nothing at all or, at best, very little indeed about the world. The *locus classicus* for his dreaming argument is René Descartes, *Meditations on First Philosophy*. In recent times, the argument has been interestingly developed by Barry Stroud in *The Significance of Philosophical Skepticism* (Oxford University Press: Oxford and New York, 1984). The "brain-in-a-vat" variant is a common contemporary version of Descartes' skeptical appeal to a powerful and deceptive "evil demon".

GEMMA is here primarily inspired by G. E. Moore, whose essay "A Defense of Common Sense" reveals in its title their fundamental shared conviction that we surely know an indefinite number of things about the world, many of them beyond the possibility of any actual or reasonable doubt. Moore's "Proof of an External World" is another well-known, challenging, and important anti-skeptical essay in the same vein. Both can be found in *G. E. Moore: Selected Writings*, Thomas Baldwin, ed. (Routledge: London, 1993).

JUSTIN spends all three conversations exploring the connection between knowledge and *justification*. The lottery problem that so exercises him in particular highlights the role of *probability* in justificatory reasoning. An important, although rather technical, early contemporary work on that topic is Henry Kyburg, *Probability and the Logic of Rational Belief* (Northwestern University Press: Evanston, IL, 1961). More recent useful discussions of lottery problem and the related "preface paradox" can be found in Richard Foley, *Working Without a Net* (Oxford University Press: Oxford and New York, 1993), and Robert J. Fogelin, *Pyrrhonian Reflections on Knowledge and Justification* (Oxford University Press: Oxford and New York, 1994).

The Second Conversation

SKIP'S "Great Car Theft Lottery" example comes from Jonathan Vogel, "Are There Counterexamples to the Closure Principle?", in Michael D. Roth and Glenn Ross, eds., *Doubting: Contemporary Perspectives on Skepticism* (Kluwer Academic Publishers: Dordrecht, Holland, 1990), pp. 13–27.

The "justified true belief" account of knowledge offered by JUSTIN goes back to Plato's *Meno* and *Theaetetus*. In the ensuing conversation, JUSTIN advocates an *externalist* view of justification, according to which beliefs are sufficiently justified if they're the outcomes of reliable causal processes, while EDIE defends the *internalist* conviction that, to be adequate for knowledge, a believer's justification be based on reasons that are epistemically available to her. The best-known externalist works are doubtless Alvin Goldman's essays "A Causal Theory of Knowing" (*Journal of Philosophy*, 64, 1967, pp. 355–72) and "Discrimination and Perceptual Knowledge" (*Journal of Philosophy*, 73, 1976, pp. 771–91), both of which have been widely reprinted. EDIE's "Nora" example is an adaptation of Keith Lehrer's "Mr. Truetemp" case in his internalist-oriented book *Theory of Knowledge* (Westview Press: Boulder, CO, 1990), where her appeal to the notion of being entitled to be confident is also more fully worked out. Useful general discussions of the internalism-externalism debate (as well as most of the other epistemological topics mentioned in the present conversations) can be found in Robert Audi, *Belief, Justification, and Knowledge* (Wadsworth Publishing Co.: Belmont, CA, 1988) and William Alston, *Epistemic Justification: Essays in the Theory of Knowledge* (Cornell University Press: Ithaca, NY, 1989).

The Third Conversation

SKIP'S "Potemkin barns" example was originally devised by Carl Ginet. In this conversation, under pressure from such cases, the internalism-externalism debate gradually gives way to the coherentism-foundationalism debate. This also has an ancient lineage, going back at least to Sextus Empiricus' outline of Agrippa's "Five Modes Leading to the Suspension of Belief" in *Outlines of Pyrrhonism*.

"Agrippa's Trilemma," as it is sometimes called, argues that justificatory appeals must ultimately issue in an infinite regress, a circle, or an ungrounded assumption. *Coherentists*, here represented by GEMMA, reject the first and third options, and attempt to base justification on closed coherent systems of reasons. Laurence BonJour's essay "The Coherence Theory of Empirical Knowledge" (*Philosophical Studies*, 30, 1976, pp. 281–312) and subsequent book, *The Structure of Empirical Knowledge* (Harvard University Press: Cambridge, MA, 1985), are among the best-known contemporary coherentist works.

In contrast, *foundationalists*, here represented by both JUSTIN and SKIP, reject the first and second horns of Agrippa's Trilemma and argue for an alternative way of grounding a set of *basic* beliefs. Roderick Chisholm's *Theory of Knowledge* 3rd ed. (Prentice-Hall, Inc.: Englewood Cliffs, NJ, 1989) offers a useful introductory account. Paul K. Moser's *Empirical Justification* (D. Reidel Publishing Co.: Dordrecht, Holland, 1985) and Richard Foley's *Working Without a Net* (see above) are articulate, contemporary foundationalist books.

EDIE's "Bruce and Betty" case, which introduces the last part of the conversation, is an example of the "Gettier problem," forcefully posed in Edmund Gettier's widely reprinted classic short essay "Is Justified True Belief Knowledge?" (*Analysis*, 26, 1963, pp. 144–6). Almost all the contemporary authors mentioned so far have something to say about the Gettier problem; indeed, many of their views are or were developed out of attempts to come to terms with it. EDIE's gruesome "Otto" story is an adaptation of one of Gilbert Harman's examples (see, e.g., his "Inference to the Best Explanation," *Philosophical Review*, 64, 1965, pp. 88–95); her "Everlight Match" example comes from Brian Skyrms (cf. "The Explication of 'X Knows that p'," *Journal of Philosophy*, 64, 1967, pp. 373–89).